A FIRST LOOK AT AMERICA'S PRESIDENTS

GEORGE WASHINGTON

The 1st President

by Josh Gregory

Consultant: Meena Bose
Director, Peter S. Kalikow Center for the Study of the American Presidency
Peter S. Kalikow Chair in Presidential Studies
Professor, Political Science
Hofstra University
Hempstead, New York

BEARPORT
PUBLISHING

New York, New York

Credits

Cover, © Painting/Alamy; 4, © Everett Collection Historical/Alamy; 5, © Joe Vogan/Alamy; 6, Centpacrr/Wikimedia Commons; 7L, © FromOldBooks.org/Alamy; 8, © North Wind Picture Archives/Alamy; 9T, Courtesy of the Library of Congress; 9B, © North Wind Picture Archives/Alamy; 10, © North Wind Picture Archives/Alamy; 11T, Courtesy of the Library of Congress; 11B, Courtesy of the Metropolitan Museum of Art/Wikimedia Commons; 12, Courtesy of the National Archives and Records Administration; 13, Courtesy of The Indian Reporter/Wikimedia Commons; 14, Courtesy of the Library of Congress; 15, © Everett Collection Inc./Alamy; 16, Courtesy of the Library of Congress; 17, Courtesy of the Library of Congress; 18, © Richard A. McMillin/Shutterstock.com; 19T, © Emma Jones/Shutterstock.com; 19BL, © Andrey Lobachev/Shutterstock.com; 19BR, © Pete Spiro/Shutterstock.com; 20, Courtesy of Centpacrr/Wikimedia Commons; 21TL, © Joe Vogan/Alamy; 21TR, Courtesy of the Library of Congress; 21B, Courtesy of The Indian Reporter/Wikimedia Commons; 22, © Jorge Salcedo/Shutterstock.com; 23BL, © Emma Jones/Shutterstock.com; 23R, Courtesy of the National Archives and Records Administration.

Publisher: Kenn Goin
Editor: Jessica Rudolph
Creative Director: Spencer Brinker
Design: The Design Lab
Photo Researcher: Josh Gregory

Special thanks to fifth-grader Lucy Barr and second-grader Brian Barr for their help in reviewing this book.

Library of Congress Cataloging-in-Publication Data

Gregory, Josh.
  George Washington: the 1st president / by Josh Gregory.
    pages cm. — (A first look at America's Presidents)
  Includes bibliographical references and index.
  Audience: Ages 5–8.
  ISBN 978-1-62724-552-4 (library binding) — ISBN 1-62724-552-9 (library binding)
  1. Washington, George, 1732-1799—Juvenile literature. 2. Presidents—United States—Biography—Juvenile literature. I. Title. II. Title: George Washington, the first president.
  E312.66.G75 2015
  973.4'1092—dc23
  [B]
                                   2014034606

For more information, write to Bearport Publishing Company, Inc., 45 West 21st Street, Suite 3B, New York, New York 10010. Printed in the United States of America.

10 9 8 7 6 5 4 3 2 1

CONTENTS

Father of a Nation

George Washington led America in the fight for freedom. He helped create the United States. As the first president, he is known as the father of our country.

Before becoming president, Washington was an important military leader.

George Wash
was presider
1789 to 17

Growing Up

George Washington was born in 1732 in Virginia. His father died when he was 11. Afterward, George helped his family. He did farmwork. He also helped take care of his younger brothers and sister.

George was born on his family's farm in Virginia.

When George was a boy, the United States did not exist. Instead, there were 13 **colonies** controlled by Great Britain. Virginia was one of the colonies.

Part of MA

Claimed by NY and NH

NH

NY

MA

PA

CT

RI

NJ

MD

DE

Virginia

NC

Atlantic Ocean

SC

GA

N W E S

13 British Colonies

Young George with his father

Off to War

In the 1750s, George Washington went off to war. Britain was fighting France for control of North America. Washington led many soldiers. He fought bravely for Britain.

In one battle, bullets tore four holes through Washington's coat. Luckily, the bullets missed his body.

Washington in a battle against the French in 1755

Washington

A battle between British and French soldiers in 1758

Britain won the war against France in 1763.

War Hero

Britain started to raise **taxes** in the colonies in the 1760s. This upset the Americans. They wanted to be free from British rule. In 1775, the Americans and the British went to war.

Washington led the American army. Thanks to his leadership, the Americans won the war.

People in the colonies spoke out against Britain and its taxes.

The war between the Americans and the British is called the Revolutionary War.

The Americans had little money to buy food and guns for the army. Washington worked hard to get these supplies for his soldiers.

Washington

In 1776, Washington led troops across the icy Delaware River for a surprise attack against the enemy.

A New Government

The United States was a new country. Its leaders needed to create a government. In 1787, Washington helped write America's **Constitution**. It tells about the country's laws. It explains how leaders are chosen.

The Constitution's words are still important today.

First President

People all over the new country looked up to Washington. He was a war hero and a great leader. Many Americans wanted him to be the nation's first president. Washington won the first presidential **election** in 1789.

People cheered for Washington after he became president.

Washington

Washington on the day he became president in 1789

In 1792, Washington was elected to another term as president. One term is four years.

A Growing Nation

Washington led the nation during a tough time. The United States was a small country with little power. While Washington was president, the country grew. Three more states became part of the nation.

Washington served as president for eight years. Then he went back to Virginia to run his farm.

Washington's home in Virginia is called Mount Vernon.

After leaving office, Washington spent time at home with his family.

Remembering Washington

Washington helped the United States become a large, powerful nation. We remember him in many ways. His face is on Mount Rushmore. The nation's **capital** is named after him.

Washington

Washington's face is carved into Mount Rushmore, in South Dakota. The other presidents shown in the sculpture are Thomas Jefferson, Theodore Roosevelt, and Abraham Lincoln.

Many people visit the Washington **Monument**. It is located in Washington, D.C.

The Washington Monument, in the nation's capital

Washington's picture is on the one-dollar bill and the quarter.

TIMELINE

**Here are some
major events from
George Washington's life.**

1732
Washington
is born in the
colony of Virginia.

1752
Washington takes over his
family's farm, known as
Mount Vernon, in Virginia.

1730   **1740**   **1750**   **1760**

1754–1763
Washington fights
for Britain in a war
against France.

1789
Washington becomes the nation's first president.

1775–1783
Washington leads the American army during the Revolutionary War.

1792
Washington is elected to a second term.

1770   1780   1790   1800

1787
Washington leads a group of Americans in creating the U.S. Constitution.

1799
Washington dies at his home.

FACTS and QUOTES

"It is better to offer no excuse than a bad one."

By the time he became president, Washington had lost all but one of his teeth. He wore false teeth made of ivory.

Washington put white powder on his hair, which was the style for men during his time.

"Every post is honorable in which a man can serve his country."

According to a legend, as a boy, Washington chopped down his father's cherry tree. When his father asked him about it, young George said, "I cannot tell a lie, Father. I cut down your cherry tree."

GLOSSARY

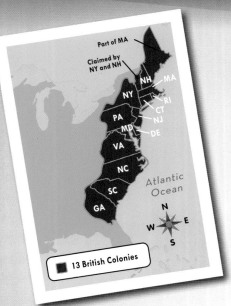

13 British Colonies

capital (KAP-uh-tuhl) the city where a country's government is located

colonies (KOL-uh-neez) areas that have been settled by people from another country and are ruled by that country

constitution (*kon*-stuh-TOO-shuhn) a document containing the basic laws of a country

election (i-LEK-shuhn) the selection of a person for office by voting

monument (MON-yuh-muhnt) a statue, building, or other structure that honors an event or person

taxes (TAKS-iz) money paid by people to the ruler or government of a country

Index

Read More

Fontes, Justine, and Ron Fontes.
*George Washington: Solider, Hero,
President (DK Readers)*. New York: DK
Publishing (2001).

Gilpin, Caroline Crosson. *George
Washington (National Geographic Kids)*.
Washington, DC: National Geographic
(2014).

Learn More Online

To learn more about George Washington, visit
www.bearportpublishing.com/AmericasPresidents

About the Author:
Josh Gregory writes
and edits books
for kids. He lives in
Chicago, Illinois.